CW01509365

Original title:
Ample Glints Amid the Fae Loft

Copyright © 2025 Swan Charm
All rights reserved.

Author: Paulina Pähkel
ISBN HARDBACK: 978-1-80562-749-4
ISBN PAPERBACK: 978-1-80564-270-1

Alight with Radiance in the Enchanted Hollow

In the hollow where shadows weave,
A glimmering light begins to breathe.
Whispers of magic fill the air,
Secrets untouched, beyond compare.

Moss carpets ground, soft and green,
Dancing beneath the silver sheen.
Stars twinkle bright, their stories unfold,
In the heart of the wood, mysteries told.

Faeries flit on wisps of breeze,
In laughter, they twirl among the trees.
Their wings like glass, bright and rare,
A symphony of joy, sweet and fair.

Moonlight bathes the world in grace,
As dreams and twilight interlace.
Hope ignites in this sacred place,
Where hearts find peace in nature's embrace.

Alight with radiance, spirits soar,
In the enchanted hollow, forevermore.

Prismatic Mists and the Faerie's Call

Through prismatic mists, soft and bright,
A faerie's voice sings in the night.
Her laughter bubbles, a sparkling stream,
A promise of wonders, a heartfelt dream.

Glistening dewdrops coat the leaves,
Nature's jewels, intricate weaves.
Each murmur of wind tells a tale,
Of hidden realms where the lost prevail.

Clouds drift lazily, shadows play,
As dawn breaks in a splendorous way.
The sky blushes with hues untold,
A tapestry woven in threads of gold.

With every step on fern-clad ground,
Magic dances silently around.
A beckoning call, so soft and clear,
The faerie whispers, "Come, linger near."

In this realm where dreams entwine,
Eternal secrets begin to shine.
With hearts wide open, we heed the thrall,
Of prismatic mists and the faerie's call.

Dappled Dreams in the Hidden Hollow

In the hollow where shadows play,
Dappled dreams drift by in the day.
Whispers carry on the breeze,
Secrets held beneath the trees.

Butterflies dance with gentle glee,
Lost in magic, wild and free.
Sunlight weaves through emerald leaves,
Weaving wonders no one believes.

The brook hums a soft, sweet rhyme,
Echoes linger, marking time.
In this haven, peace resides,
Where the world and dreams collide.

Twilight's Embrace in the Arcane Woods

As twilight falls, the woods transform,
Stars awaken, bright and warm.
Mystic creatures stir and sigh,
Underneath the starlit sky.

Moonbeams dance on ancient stone,
Whispers echo, not alone.
Flickering flames in hidden glades,
Reveal the magic that never fades.

Covered paths where shadows roam,
Offer secrets, far from home.
In this embrace, hearts take flight,
Chasing dreams in the quiet night.

Enchanted Light over Yonder Hill

Over yonder hill, a glow,
A tapestry of dawn's soft flow.
Colors burst, a painter's dream,
As day awakens with a beam.

Fields of gold and skies of blue,
Nature's brush, such vibrant hue.
Laughter lingers on the air,
As creatures play without a care.

In every blossom, a story told,
A world of wonders to behold.
Hope rises with the morning light,
Guiding hearts into the bright.

Glowing Secrets in the Wooded Glimmer

In the forest where secrets hide,
Glowing glimmers softly bide.
Fireflies blink like stars gone wild,
In the arms of night, beguiled.

Mossy nooks and quiet streams,
Whisper of forgotten dreams.
Branches sway, a sweet refrain,
Crafting magic in the rain.

Every shadow, every glance,
Holds within a whispered chance.
Nature's heart beats strong and true,
In this glimmer, old and new.

Sparkling Currents in the Faerie's Stream

A glimmer dances on the wave,
Where faeries weave, a world to save.
With whispered songs that light the night,
They guide the lost with gentle light.

Beneath the boughs, where shadows play,
They spin their dreams, both night and day.
A splash of joy, a twinkle's gleam,
Unraveling the fabric of a dream.

The ripples hold a tale untold,
Of silver fish and treasures bold.
They swim through laughter, swirl in glee,
Their sparkle bright as magic's spree.

In silken streams where wishes flow,
The currents sing, the breezes blow.
Each droplet sings of joy and cheer,
In faerie realms, where time's unclear.

So come, dear friend, and take a dive,
In sparkling waters, feel alive.
The faerie's stream, a wondrous sight,
Where hearts can soar and dreams take flight.

Chasing Shadows of Luminescent Fantasies

In moonlit woods where shadows twine,
The whispers weave, both dark and fine.
A chase begins, through leafy plays,
Where shadows dance in misty rays.

Each flicker hides a tale so sweet,
With secrets where the wild things meet.
A flickering spark, a fleeting glance,
In luminescence, we take our chance.

Through tangled branches, spirits glide,
In visions bright, we dare to bide.
The dreams that pulse in quiet hum,
Paint stories of where we come from.

With every step, a breath of night,
As twinkling stars lend softest light.
We chase the hues of what could be,
In luminescent reverie.

So follow softly, heed the call,
To shadows deep, where night can fall.
In fantasies, forever roam,
The chase ignites, we find our home.

The Monarch's Path of Shimmering Dust

On winding trails where whispers soar,
The monarch walks, his heart the core.
A path adorned with glittering gold,
Each step a story waiting to unfold.

In jeweled light, the shadows gleam,
A sovereign's dream within a dream.
With wings of grace, he sweeps the land,
A ruler's touch by fate's own hand.

From flower blooms to mountain high,
The shimmering dust ignites the sky.
A dance of colors, bright and bold,
Their beauty speaks of legends told.

O'er crystal streams, where wishes rise,
The paths of dreams reflect the skies.
Each whispered hope, a promise made,
In monarch's light, no fear can wade.

So tread the path where shimmer leads,
In golden threads, plant joyful seeds.
The monarch's way, where dreams take flight,
In shimmering dust, we find the light.

Echoes of Luster in the Verdant Vale

In valleys rich with emerald hue,
The echoes speak of tales so true.
With laughter light and gentle sighs,
A symphony beneath the skies.

Through rustling leaves, the whispers flow,
With secrets only nature knows.
In every breeze, a soft embrace,
In verdant vale, we find our place.

The luster shines on petals pure,
In every heart, a sweet allure.
With timeless charms, the valley sings,
Of magic born in fleeting things.

Each turn reveals a hidden bliss,
A world where dreams and daylight kiss.
In echoes filled with life's caress,
We wander on, our hearts confess.

So step with soft, deliberate grace,
In verdant vale, we find our space.
With echoes of luster, kindly shared,
The beauty of life—eternally bared.

Ephemeral Glimmers in the Midnight Wood

In shadows deep where whispers weave,
The silver moon casts dreams that cleave.
Amongst the leaves, a soft light glows,
A transient dance, where magic flows.

With every step, the heart must race,
As glimmers fade, time leaves no trace.
The nightingale sings a haunting tune,
While stars embrace the sleeping moon.

The forest sighs, a sacred ground,
Where secrets shared are seldom found.
A flicker here, a spark of hope,
In midnight's arms, we learn to cope.

A fleeting smile, a gentle touch,
In twilight's realm, we long for much.
Yet, all that shines is bound to cease,
In fleeting moments, we find peace.

Caress of Light in the Faerie's Palm

Beneath the boughs where fairies play,
A whisper speaks, then fades away.
In silver beams, their laughter twirls,
A sacred space where magic swirls.

Soft glimmers rest in gentle hands,
As evening's breath caresses lands.
In faerie's palm, the world seems bright,
Each twinkle holds a shard of light.

With every word, the starlight bends,
As time suspends, and dreams transcend.
The moonlit path, a woven thread,
In twilight's book, the heart is led.

A sigh of wonder graces the air,
In faerie's realm, we shed our care.
Where shadows dance and spirits gleam,
In twilight's glow, we find our dream.

Glistening Echoes in the Fern's Embrace

In glades where ferns in silence sway,
The echoes move, then drift away.
A shimmering light on dewy leaves,
In nature's arms, the heart believes.

With every rustle, tales unfold,
Of ancient woods and spirits bold.
The gentle breeze hums low and sweet,
Where earth and sky in rapture meet.

Each glistening drop reflects the stars,
As night-time whispers blur the scars.
In emerald depths, a magic swells,
The forest sings what silence tells.

A tender hush, a patient pause,
In ferns we find the world's applause.
With open hearts, we breathe it in,
In nature's clasp, our souls begin.

Silvery Threads of Enchanted Time

In twilight's loom, the threads align,
With silken strands of fate's design.
Each moment caught in moonlit weave,
A tapestry of dreams we believe.

The clock ticks slow in gentle nights,
As shadows blend with soft starlights.
The past and future intertwine,
In whispered tales, the ages shine.

With every stitch, the stories shift,
In hours carved from time's great rift.
Ephemeral, yet deeply felt,
In every heartbeat, magic dwelt.

So linger not in moments lost,
For life's a thread, though we exhaust.
Embrace the flow, let it entwine,
In silvery dreams, let our hearts align.

Ethereal Wonders in the Faery Wilds

In the heart of the whispering trees,
Where the moonlight spills like dreams,
Faery laughter dances in the breeze,
Each sparkle bursting at the seams.

Glow of lanterns, soft and bright,
Guiding footsteps through the mist,
A dance of shadows in the night,
In secrets shared, none dare to resist.

Petals woven with silver thread,
Upon the brook, where wishes sing,
In twilight's glow, the world we tread,
Awakens hope in everything.

Whispers of tales in ancient stone,
Echo the wisdom of the skies,
In the faery wilds, we are never alone,
For magic thrives where imagination flies.

Dance of the Stardust Spheres

In the hush of the velvet night,
Stars twirl in a cosmic waltz,
They shimmer and spin with pure delight,
In the silence, there are no faults.

Each flicker, a note in celestial song,
Guiding travelers lost in their dreams,
As echoes of time weave memories strong,
Lighting the paths of moonlit beams.

Nebulas bloom in colors ablaze,
Painting the heavens with hues so bold,
The dance of the spheres, a timeless phase,
Revealing the stories of ages old.

In the tapestry of endless night,
We find our place, our cosmic birth,
In stardust whispers, hearts take flight,
Unraveling secrets of the universe's worth.

Shimmering Threads of the Evernight

In the fabric of night, threads intertwine,
Glistening secrets in shadows cast,
Each stitch a heartbeat, a pulse divine,
In the evernight, magic holds fast.

Luminous glimmers weave through the dark,
Lighting the corners where silence dwells,
Echoes of dreams, each flicker a spark,
Creating whispers that time compels.

Veils of twilight, soft and deep,
Cradle the moments we cherish and live,
In their embrace, the stars seem to weep,
For the dreams we sow, the love we give.

In the dance of the shadows, stories unfold,
With every shimmer, a journey begins,
The threads of the night have magic untold,
Binding our hearts in luminous skins.

Veil of Illumination in Fae Transience

Beneath the veil of shimmering light,
Fae enchantment weaves through the air,
Ethereal glimmers, a fleeting sight,
An invitation to dream and dare.

Moments of wonder float like a sigh,
Brushing the surface of thoughts unclear,
In the quiet, a lullaby,
Awakening hopes that whisper near.

Twinkling orbs of ethereal grace,
Flit like shadows in playful delight,
Through timeless realms, we find our place,
In the dance of day turning into night.

In this dance of the fae, we glean,
The beauty of life's ephemeral song,
Caught in the spell of the unseen,
Embracing the magic where we belong.

Chimeras in Twilight's Embrace

In twilight's hush, where shadows dance,
Chimeras weave their mystic trance.
With glimmers bright and whispers low,
They guard the secrets we can't know.

Beneath the arc of fading light,
Their forms emerge, a splendid sight.
With wings of gold and eyes that gleam,
They draw us into a vivid dream.

A flickering heart, a fleeting sigh,
They soar on winds, both low and high.
In every breath, a tale unfolds,
Of magic lost and daring bold.

Through emerald glades, their laughter rings,
As night unfurls its velvet strings.
Enchanted woods, they roam so free,
In dreams they live, so wild and free.

So close your eyes, let visions flow,
Into the dusk where chimeras go.
In twilight's arms, let your spirit chase,
The wonders found in twilight's embrace.

Luminescent Dreams of the Woodland Court

In the heart of woods where fairies dwell,
Luminescent dreams cast a spell.
The moonlight dances on silken streams,
Awakening the whispers of dreams.

With every step on the forest floor,
Secrets linger behind every door.
A shimmering glow, a gentle sigh,
In dreams of the woodland, time drifts by.

In silvery beams, the stories unfold,
Of quests for the brave and tales of old.
Magic weaves through the branches above,
In the softest caress of nature's love.

Here, stars twinkle in green-lit skies,
And every rustling leaf softly sighs.
A court of wonder, a realm of grace,
In luminescent dreams, we find our place.

So wander deep where the wild things play,
In the woodland court, let your heart sway.
With each glowing step, let your spirit soar,
In the dreams of the woods, forevermore.

Flickers of Magic in Twilight's Garden

In twilight's garden, where shadows play,
Flickers of magic bloom and sway.
With petals soft and colors bright,
They whisper secrets of the night.

Each twinkling star, a guardian's gaze,
Lighting the path through the evening haze.
In this haven where wildflowers grow,
The pulse of the earth begins to glow.

Breezes carry a fragrant tune,
Beneath the watch of the silver moon.
A dance of fireflies, a glimmering show,
In the heart of the garden, enchantments flow.

With every thrum of the nightingale's song,
The spirit of magic is never wrong.
In twilight's embrace, let your soul ignite,
With flickers of wonder, pure and bright.

So linger long where dreams reside,
In the garden where mysteries hide.
For in every glance, a story weaves,
In the flickers of magic, our heart believes.

Ethereal Radiance of Enchanted Realms

In realms enchanted, where starlight glows,
Ethereal radiance softly flows.
With whispers sweet that call the brave,
To lands where the heart learns how to waive.

Through crystal streams that shimmer bright,
Adventurers seek the fading light.
Each step unveils a world anew,
In riddles of old, where dreams come true.

The ancient trees, they sway and sigh,
Beneath the vast and endless sky.
With every breath, magic intertwines,
In the ether where the cosmos shines.

A tapestry woven with threads of delight,
In enchanted realms, dreams take flight.
With every star, a story sparks,
In the ethereal realm, the magicarks.

So venture forth where the spirit flies,
In the glow of the night, let your heart rise.
In the radiance found in these blessed fields,
The ethereal secrets, the heart reveals.

Celestial Whispers on the Wind

In starlit skies, the secrets flow,
Whispers carried where moonlight glows.
Each breeze a tale of long-lost time,
Echoes soft in a rhythmic rhyme.

Night's gentle arms embrace the light,
As shadows dance with the spirit's flight.
Stars twinkle bright, their stories unfold,
In silver threads of the night so bold.

Every sigh of the wandering breeze,
Holds ancient dreams of the night's tease.
While constellations muse and gleam,
In the heart of darkness, they brightly beam.

Awake, the world in twilight's gleam,
In every whisper, we dare to dream.
The wind carries truths, both new and old,
Of love and longing yet untold.

So listen close, to the wind's sweet call,
In celestial realms, we rise and fall.
For in the quiet, where shadows blend,
Are the whispers of hope that never end.

Fables of Light in Woodland Ambers

In dappled light where the forest breathes,
Nature hums with ancient wreaths.
Beneath the boughs, the stories grow,
In every rustle, in every flow.

Amber hues in the sunset glow,
Whispering fables only trees know.
With each stride on the mossy ground,
Magic stirs in silence profound.

Squirrels chatter in playful glee,
While shadows stretch beneath each tree.
Rabbits hop with quivering ears,
As twilight falls and darkness nears.

The brook babbles of secrets kept,
While fireflies weave, as dreamers slept.
In the embrace of the woodland fair,
We find our tales floating in the air.

So wander deep where fables rise,
In whispers soft beneath the skies.
For every leaf that dances free,
Holds the spirit of mystery.

Enchanted Reflections on Crystal Waters

Beneath the surface, the world is still,
Mirrored dreams on a silver chill.
Ripples trace the outlines bright,
As magic sways in the moon's soft light.

Reflections hold the whispers near,
Of hopes and wishes cast sincere.
In every ripple, stories twine,
In crystal waters where hearts align.

The lily blooms with delicate grace,
In tranquil waters, it finds its place.
While fish weave patterns, swift and free,
In the tapestry of the deep green sea.

With every splash, secrets break,
We gather dreams that water makes.
In the sacred pool where spirits blend,
Is a dance of light that knows no end.

So dip your fingers in the clear,
And feel the pulse of dreams held dear.
For in these waters, a realm so vast,
We find reflections of the past.

Luminous Reveries in Fairybound Dreams

In twilight's grasp, where fairies play,
Luminous whispers call us to stay.
Amidst the blooms, in the evening glow,
Reveries weave where enchantments flow.

With every flutter of gossamer wings,
A symphony of magic softly sings.
In fantasy realms where wishes gleam,
We dance upon the edge of a dream.

Moonlit paths of a sparkling hue,
Guide lost souls to the magic true.
In wonder's grip, we twirl and spin,
Where the heart believes, the dreams begin.

Each glance around holds a charm to share,
In luminous realms, our spirits flare.
With laughter ringing in the night's embrace,
We find our joy in this secret place.

So let your heart take flight on wings,
As darkness falls, and adventure springs.
For in these dreams, the world aligns,
In luminous realms, where magic shines.

Secrets of the Sylphs in the Twilight

In twilight's hush, the whispers dwell,
With secrets spun from air's soft spell.
The sylphs in dance, a graceful flight,
Weaving dreams from the strands of night.

Their laughter twirls in the velvet dark,
The shimmering glow, a fleeting spark.
With every flutter, the shadows play,
Guardians of dusk, they guide the way.

Through misty glades, where shadows loom,
They beckon forth the stars to bloom.
In hidden realms, where magic brews,
The sylphs unveil their ancient clues.

Soft breezes whisper, tales of yore,
Of fae and sprites on the forest floor.
With gossamer wings, they drift and sway,
In twilight's grasp, they softly stay.

So heed the call when evening's near,
For in the twilight, their song is clear.
The secrets shared in a moonlit trance,
Invite your heart to join their dance.

Soft Ray Dreams Beneath Branching Boughs

In realms where sunlight kisses the ground,
Soft rays of gold in the silence found.
Beneath the boughs, a sheltered dream,
Whispers of magic, like a gentle stream.

The leaves above, a canopy bright,
Craft shadows that flicker with morning light.
Here lies a world where worries cease,
A tranquil haven, a space of peace.

Birds serenade in a lilting tune,
As petals dance beneath the silvery moon.
In this fragrant nook, time slows its flight,
And worries melt like mist in the night.

With each soft ray, a story unfolds,
Of love and friendship in amber and gold.
The heart takes wing in this sacred place,
In soft ray dreams, we find our grace.

Nestled in roots, dreams intertwine,
As branches sway to a rhythm divine.
Beneath the boughs, a glance will show,
The wonders hidden that softly glow.

Twilight's Lullaby of the Glimmering Grove

As twilight descends on the glimmering leaves,
A lullaby whispers through swaying eaves.
The grove holds secrets in shadows so deep,
Where fairies and sprites in their twilight leap.

With hushed melodies, the world quiets down,
A magical realm where dreams wear a crown.
Ethereal lights dance in the evening's embrace,
In twilight's lullaby, we find our place.

The crescent moon bathes the grove in her glow,
Her light weaves a tapestry, radiant and slow.
With each lilting note, the stars ignite,
Filling the heart with pure delight.

Let go of the day, release all your sighs,
In the hush of twilight, the spirit flies.
A chorus of crickets begins their refrain,
Marking the end of a sunlit reign.

So linger a moment beneath the soft trees,
And breathe in the magic on the gentle breeze.
For in this embrace, where shadows merge,
The lullaby sings, inviting the urge.

The Flicker of Sunlit Spells

A flicker of spells in the morning light,
Whispers of magic take wondrous flight.
The sun casts gold on the waking earth,
In every sparkle, a hint of rebirth.

Through dewdrops glisten, the forest wakes,
Soft murmurs rise in the midst of lakes.
The dance of the leaves in the gentle breeze,
Awakens the heart with enchanting ease.

With every heartbeat, the magic flows,
In beams of sunshine, a secret grows.
The world is alive, vibrant and bright,
As spells of the sun weave day from night.

So wander where shadows mingle with light,
Where each flicker brings dreams to sight.
Embrace the warmth as the morning swells,
Where life and wonder invoke sunlit spells.

Whispers of Light Beneath the Canopy

In the deep woods, shadows play,
Softly where the night meets day.
Luminous whispers weave through trees,
Carried gently on the breeze.

Stars shimmer in the velvet sky,
While silver streams of laughter sigh.
Nature sings her quiet song,
In this realm where hearts belong.

Mossy carpets cradle the ground,
While creatures dance without a sound.
Moonlit paths invite the brave,
To seek the dreams that magic gave.

In every rustle, secrets hide,
In shadowed corners, fairies glide.
With twinkling eyes and knowing grins,
Beneath the leaves, adventure begins.

Hold your breath, in silence dwell,
Every heartbeat casts a spell.
Amongst the whispers of the night,
Find your truth in beams of light.

Shimmering Echoes in the Enchanted Grove

Echoes dance through ancient trees,
A melody carried on the breeze.
Sunlight filters through the boughs,
Kissing petals, sacred vows.

Glistening dew on every leaf,
Nature's beauty, beyond belief.
Mystic visions swirl and twine,
In this grove where dreams align.

Roots entwined, a tale unfolds,
Of whispered love, of laughter bold.
Crickets serenade the night,
In the hush, find pure delight.

Wandering spirits glide and spin,
In the echoes, let peace begin.
A tapestry of sound and light,
Awaits your heart beneath the night.

Follow the path to secrets deep,
Where the ancient trees still keep.
In each shimmer, find your place,
In the echo of nature's grace.

Secrets Danced in the Moonlit Glade

In the glade where shadows sway,
Moonlight sparkles, guiding the way.
Secrets whispered on the night air,
Luring dreamers, so beware.

Softly rustling, leaves applaud,
A serenade to nature's god.
In this realm, twilight weaves,
Tales of magic that never leaves.

Bright-eyed sprites twirl in delight,
Chasing flames of fireflies bright.
Barefoot dancers twine and spin,
In the heart where wonders begin.

The cool breeze sings of stories past,
As time's sweet grip is ever cast.
In the glade, let secrets flow,
In moonlit charms, what dreams bestow.

Hold your breath and feel the thrill,
Every heartbeat echoes still.
Between the shadows, find your soul,
In the glade, become whole.

Glistening Dreams in the Woodland Realm

In the woodland, dreams take flight,
Bathed in warmth of soft starlight.
Glistening paths of emerald hue,
Invite the heart to venture through.

Whispers linger on the breeze,
As magic dances 'neath the trees.
A symphony of night unfolds,
In every story that nature holds.

Crimson blooms and silver ferns,
Twilight glimmers as the world turns.
In this realm of pure enchant,
Dare to dream, let spirits chant.

Hold the secrets close and tight,
In shadows cast by gentle light.
The woodland hums a peaceful song,
In each rustle, you belong.

Let your heart soar, leap, and play,
Through hidden paths where fairies stay.
In the woodland realm, you will find,
Glistening dreams that free the mind.

Flickers of Magic in the Sylvan Shadows

In the woods where whispers dwell,
Lurking shadows weave their spell.
A shimmer bright, a fleeting glance,
Inviting hearts to join the dance.

Moonlight glimmers on the leaves,
Stirring dreams that fate weaves.
Softly calling with a sigh,
In this realm where spirits fly.

Echoes linger in the night,
Casting spells with pure delight.
Twinkling lights like fireflies,
Guide lost wanderers 'neath the skies.

Ancient oaks and stone-cold springs,
Guard the secrets nature brings.
Through the mist, a laughter twirls,
As the magic softly unfurls.

Time stands still in whispered lore,
Where every heart can dream and soar.
In this realm, our souls ignite,
Flickers of dreams in silver light.

Fairy Lanterns and Starry Smiles

Beneath the arch of twilight's grace,
Fairies gather, each tiny face.
With lanterns aglow, they spin and twirl,
Weaving light in a wondrous whirl.

Stars above wink with delight,
As gentle wings take to flight.
Through the meadows, adventure calls,
Echoing in the moonlit halls.

Softly singing, a melody sweet,
Bringing joy to every heartbeat.
Enchanting whispers in the night air,
Reminding us magic is always there.

In every step, in every sigh,
The world is painted by dreams gone by.
Smiles like stardust linger long,
In the rhythm of a fairy's song.

Join the dance, feel the thrill,
Embrace the night and let time still.
With fairy lanterns held up high,
We'll chase the dreams that light the sky.

Ethereal Radiance in the Twilight Thicket

In the thicket where shadows weave,
Ethereal light bids us believe.
Crickets hum a tender tune,
Under the watchful eye of the moon.

Veils of mist gently rise and swirl,
Unraveling secrets in the world.
Flashes of color, soft and bright,
A festival glows, pure and light.

Dreams take wing on silken air,
Carried forth without a care.
Each flicker deepens the night's delight,
Filling hearts with purest light.

The twilight whispers a tale of old,
Of bravery, of magic untold.
In this sanctuary of the wild,
Nature's essence leaves us beguiled.

As starlight drapes the dancing trees,
We're all embraced by gentle breeze.
In ethereal radiance, we find our way,
Guided by night until the day.

Illuminated Paths of the Sprite's Journey

Follow the path where the sprite did roam,
In every corner lies a home.
Glimmers trace the steps of grace,
Through enchanted realms they embrace.

With laughter echoing through the glen,
With stories told again and again.
Tiny wings in a joyful flutter,
Sprinkling magic, soft as butter.

Among the blooms, in shadows deep,
The sprites awaken from their sleep.
Guiding travelers with a glowing light,
Illuminating dreams, pure and bright.

Each moment shared whispers a tune,
Harvesting joy from dawn till moon.
Within the leaves and dewdrop's gleam,
The world unfolds like a tender dream.

So walk the trails lit by playful sprites,
Discover hidden wonders in the nights.
With every twinkle, every glance,
Life is magic, calling us to dance.

Embrace the journey, take the chance,
For every heartbeat holds a romance.
Along illuminated paths so free,
The sprites invite you, come and see.

Mysteries Wrapped in Dew-Kissed Petals

In the garden where shadows play,
Petals whisper secrets of the day.
Each drop of dew, a story spun,
Of magic hidden, waiting to be won.

Blossoms cling to the morning light,
Cradling dreams in colors bright.
With every breeze, a tale will dance,
Inviting hearts to take a chance.

Beneath the petals, worlds unseen,
Where fairies flit and prisms gleam.
A tapestry in shades of grace,
Beckoning souls to this wondrous place.

Each fragrance drifts, a call to roam,
Through labyrinth paths that lead us home.
In the quiet, magic stirs,
A symphony of life that purrs.

Beneath the arch of ancient trees,
Hope is carried on the breeze.
With every bloom, a promise made,
In the heart of the garden's shade.

The Serene Glow of Fabled Grove

In twilight's hush, the grove awakes,
Whispers soft as the river's lakes.
Moonlight drips from leaves so fair,
Glimmers dance in the cool night air.

The ancient trees, with stories wide,
Guard the secrets that they bide.
Each rustle tells of years gone by,
Holding truths that never die.

Fireflies weave through the dusky haze,
Like stars reborn in amber ways.
Underneath the watchful skies,
Nature beckons with gentle sighs.

Crickets sing of magic's reign,
In the silence, echoes remain.
The grove, a realm of dreams and lore,
Calls us forth, forevermore.

With every step, a mystery found,
In the rustling of leaves all around.
As shadows gather in soft repose,
The fabled grove in stillness glows.

Starlight Lingers in Hidden Glens

In hallowed glens where starlight weaves,
Nightly tales, like silver leaves.
Beneath the canvas, vast and deep,
Whispers of the night, secrets keep.

A gentle sigh of twilight breeze,
Carries dreams upon the seas.
Each twinkling star a wish fulfilled,
In hidden nooks where hopes are thrilled.

Shadows dance, their secrets blend,
Time in stillness, and love can mend.
The air is thick with magic's grace,
Inviting all to this sacred space.

In the quiet, tranquility flows,
Guiding the heart where serendipity goes.
The night unfolds, a soft embrace,
In hidden glens, we find our place.

As dawn's first light begins to break,
Hope springs forth with every ache.
Yet in the hush, we know it's true,
Starlight lingers, forever new.

Reflections of Wonder in Sylvan Pools

Beside the pools where lilies sway,
Reflections whisper the song of day.
Mirrors of dreams, still waters hold,
Stories waiting to be told.

In verdant realms where echoes meet,
The air is laced with scents so sweet.
A world beneath, so rich, so bright,
Captured glimmers of evening light.

Ripples dance with the moon's soft gleam,
Bringing to life each waking dream.
Nature cradles the heart's own tune,
Guiding souls to the silver moon.

Amidst the reeds, the whispers play,
Each moment cherished, never fray.
In the deep, a serenade swirls,
Revealing treasures of hidden worlds.

With every glance, a wonder caught,
In sylvan pools where peace is sought.
Here, reflection paints the skies anew,
Lost in reverie, forever true.

Celestial Beams Among the Mossy Stones

In twilight's grace, the shadows play,
While whispers of stars drift softly away.
Mossy stones bask in the moon's kind light,
Guarding all secrets hidden from sight.

A gentle hush holds the ancients near,
The echo of magic dances in air.
Celestial beams weave through each leaf,
Binding the world in a fleeting belief.

Where twilight meets the day's last sigh,
The heart of the forest begins to fly.
Each moment glimmers, each breath a song,
In this enchanted place, we all belong.

Pale fireflies flicker, their laughter rings,
A symphony woven with delicate strings.
The mountains cradle the dreams of the night,
As shadows embrace the bold and the bright.

So linger awhile on this mossy nest,
Where time holds its breath, and hearts find their rest.
With celestial beams lighting the way,
We dance with the magic, come what may.

Luminescence in the Gossamer Veil

Under the moon's soft, shimmering veil,
Whispers of magic in the night prevail.
Gossamer threads of dreams interlace,
A tapestry woven in silvery grace.

The nightingale sings to the rising dawn,
As daybreak's glow paints the world reborn.
Each droplet of dew, a crystal clear sight,
Reflecting the wonders of endless night.

In the forest's embrace, shadows entwine,
Stars peek through branches where moonbeams shine.
An ethereal glow bathes the ancient trees,
In secrets held close by the murmuring breeze.

A dance of fireflies in harmony glows,
Like scattered wishes where the river flows.
Each flicker a promise, each shimmer a dream,
In luminescence, life flows like a stream.

So let your heart wander through this fair land,
Where every soft glimmer is carefully planned.
Beneath the gossamer veil, secrets conceal,
The magic of night, a wondrous appeal.

Sprightly Glimmers by the Forest Stream

By the forest stream where the wildflowers sway,
Sprightly glimmers chase all shadows away.
Rippling laughter flows over the stone,
A melody sweet, not meant to be lone.

Beneath the bright canopy, whispers take flight,
Each flower unfurls to embrace the light.
Sunbeams dance lightly on water's smooth glass,
While stories of ages in ripples will pass.

The brook's gentle babble, a song of its own,
Carries the secrets of time nearly flown.
In moments enchanted, the world melts away,
While the forest delights in its whims of play.

Chasing the sparkles that twinkle and shine,
With every new step, the forest aligns.
In this sacred space where dreams softly gleam,
Hold tight to the magic, let your heart dream.

So linger awhile by the stream's gentle sigh,
Where sprightly glimmers invite you to fly.
Nature's embrace, a soft, loving seam,
Binds us together in a beautiful dream.

Dance of Light in the Verdant Hollow

In a verdant hollow where the wild things play,
A dance of light welcomes the end of day.
Sunset's warm touch coats the leaves in gold,
As stories of nature's wonders unfold.

Each tiny flicker, a spark from above,
Whispers of magic and whispers of love.
The branches sway gently in a soft breeze,
As soft as the heartbeats of waking trees.

Moonbeams cascade through the emerald glades,
Illuminating paths where the twilight cascades.
The laughter of spirits joins celestial cheer,
In every soft sigh, their happiness clear.

With twinkling stars winking in darkening air,
The dance of light weaves through everywhere.
A symphony bright, a harmonious song,
Fills the heart's chamber, invites you along.

So rest here awhile, breathe the sweet night,
Embrace the dance of the fading light.
In this verdant hollow, where magic is found,
The heartbeat of nature sings all around.

Breaths of Light in the Eldergrove

In shadows deep, the whispers play,
Where ancient trees keep night at bay.
A shimmer soft, a glimmer bright,
Breaths of warmth, in gentle light.

Through emerald leaves, the sunbeams dance,
In every nook, there's magic's chance.
With laughter soft, the spirits glide,
In Eldergrove, where dreams abide.

A path of gold, through dew-kissed blooms,
In nature's arms, all fear consumes.
The air is sweet, the heart feels free,
In this enchanted tapestry.

With every step, the stories weave,
Of woodland's grace, in sighs we believe.
Lost in wonder, the moments flow,
In breaths of light, our spirits grow.

Misty Hues Beyond the Faerie Ring

In twilight's hush, a veil descends,
Where magic winds and time suspends.
A faerie ring in mossy glade,
In misty hues, the dreams cascade.

Secrets whisper on the breeze,
Upon the boughs of ancient trees.
With glimmering eyes, the fae take flight,
In shimmering veils of silver light.

A world unbound by mortal's time,
Where melodies of hearts do chime.
In every smile, a spell of old,
Misty hues in stories told.

The moon descends on velvet nights,
Casting shadows, soft and bright.
In laughter sweet, the echoes ring,
As dreams arise beyond the ring.

Radiant Dreams Twined with Moonbeams

In silken threads of twilight hue,
Radiant dreams, in starlight's view.
With every sigh, the night unfolds,
Stories whispered, secrets told.

Moonbeams dance on silver streams,
Woven softly into dreams.
In shadows cast, the magic stirs,
As quiet hearts, the night endures.

A fleeting time, where wishes bloom,
In radiant glows, dispels the gloom.
With every glance, the stars align,
As dreams entwine with the divine.

Through whispered winds and velvet skies,
In every moment, timeless sighs.
The world awakens, breathes anew,
In dreams aglow, where hearts accrue.

The Glorious Radiance of Nature's Sorrow

In twilight's shade, where shadows creep,
Nature weeps, her secrets deep.
A glorious radiance unfolds,
In every petal, story holds.

Through blossoms bright, the tears do flow,
In every breeze, a tale of woe.
Yet beauty blooms in pain's embrace,
The earth's lament, a tender grace.

In stillness reigns, a haunting song,
Of bittersweet where hearts belong.
With each soft sigh, the world unites,
In nature's sorrow, hidden delights.

The mountains stand, with heads held high,
While rivers weep, beneath the sky.
In every shadow, light will find,
A glorious path, to heal mankind.

Spellbound Moments in Moonlit Whispers

In twilight's embrace, shadows weave,
A tapestry rich, of dreams we conceive.
With whispers soft, the night holds sway,
As magic dances 'til break of day.

Stars like diamonds, twinkle and gleam,
Unraveling secrets, the heart's quiet dream.
Each pulse of the night, a mystical heartbeat,
In moonlit whispers, where worlds softly meet.

Beneath silver skies, we gather and sigh,
Old tales spinning 'neath the night's watchful eye.
A flicker of light, with soft velvet touch,
In spellbound moments, we linger so much.

Echoes of laughter, the night softly sings,
A waltz through the night, on enchanted wings.
Each sigh and laugh, a spell that's rehearsed,
In the glow of the moon, where all hearts are cursed.

So let us remain in this dreamlike trance,
With the moonlight as guide, and magic in dance.
For every whisper, a promise anew,
In spellbound moments, my heart belongs to you.

The Enchantment of Silvered Dewdrops

Dewdrops glisten on the dawn's embrace,
Whispers of night leave a silvery trace.
In breath of morning, soft secrets unfurl,
Awakening dreams in a luminous whirl.

Each drop a pearl, a moment in time,
Caught in the light, a crystalline rhyme.
As sunlight spills over the slumbering grass,
Nature's enchantments, in silence, amass.

With every shimmer, a tale softly spun,
Of fleeting moments, when night's all but done.
The world awakens, and with it, a glow,
In the heart of the meadow, the magic will flow.

Each blade a canvas, an artist's delight,
The dewdrops twinkle, a dazzling sight.
Like wishes from fairies, they glint and they shine,
In the enchantment of morning, our hearts intertwine.

So pause for a moment, in joy and in peace,
Embrace the enchantment, let all worries cease.
For silvered dewdrops catch dreams in their flight,
An enchanting glimpse of the morning light.

Magic Flickers Beneath Shaded Foliage

In the forest's heart, where shadows play,
Magic flickers, hidden from day.
With leaves that whisper tales from the past,
Every rustle and sigh, a spell is cast.

Sunbeams dance through the emerald leaves,
Weaving gold threads in the fabric it weaves.
Beneath canopies deep, our secrets we keep,
In the hush of the woods, where memories sleep.

Creatures of wonder glide in the mist,
Eyes full of promise, not to be missed.
In nooks and crannies, tales come alive,
As magic unfolds, and the spirits thrive.

Follow the glow where the fireflies twirl,
In shadowy corners, let the adventure unfurl.
Each flutter, a spark of the wild unknown,
In places forgotten, where fantasy's grown.

So linger awhile, in this verdant retreat,
Where magic flickers and day feels complete.
In the heart of the forest, let dreams take their flight,
For beneath shaded foliage, there's purest delight.

Glistening Hues of the Wildflower Meadow

In wildflower meadows, colors collide,
A symphony bright, where secrets abide.
Petals of gold, and violet hues,
Nature's own brush, painting endless views.

The dance of the breeze, a soft serenade,
Each blossom a note in the wild masquerade.
Amidst the tall grasses, murmurs arise,
As butterflies flit in their delicate guise.

Laughter of bees, with their jubilant song,
They weave through the petals, where they belong.
In fragrant embrace, the daylight will play,
In glistening hues, chasing shadows away.

Beneath broader skies, we lay in repose,
Surrounded by beauty, the heart gently knows.
Each moment a treasure, a memory spun,
In wildflower meadows, two hearts beat as one.

So here in the splendor, let worries dissolve,
Amidst colors vibrant, our spirits evolve.
In the gift of the meadow, where we can roam free,
Glistening hues cradle, our souls in harmony.

Twinkling Fairies in the Secret Glade

In the heart of the night, soft whispers lie,
Twinkling fairies dance, under the sky.
Their laughter like music, a light fragile breeze,
They weave their enchantments among ancient trees.

With petals aglow, they flit and they dart,
Each flicker of light, a piece of their heart.
Beneath moonlit branches, they gather in throngs,
To share secret tales, in melodious songs.

The secretive glade, a realm woven fine,
Where dreams take their flight on the silken vine.
Fairies spin wishes, like threads of pure gold,
In their enchanted world, where magic unfolds.

By glimmering streams, where reflections play,
The spirit of night softly guides their ballet.
In harmony blooming, they dance with delight,
Painting the shadows with soft beams of light.

So if ever you wander, where twilight descends,
Listen closely for laughter, where twilight amends.
For in the deep woods, where time stands apart,
Twinkling fairies await, to gather your heart.

Mirage of Stars in the Woodland Canopy

Under the vastness of a velvet night,
Stars whisper secrets, distant and bright.
Through the woodland canopy, magic unfolds,
Mirroring dreams that the universe holds.

Each glimmering beacon, a wish set adrift,
Guiding lost souls through the starlight's soft lift.
Nature's own tapestry, woven with care,
Encasing the whispers spun from the air.

Moonlight dances softly on leaves made of lace,
Illuminating paths in this mystical space.
Creatures of wonder, on silent night's wings,
Join in the symphony that the nighttime brings.

Glimmers of magic cascade from above,
Like dreams set afloat on the currents of love.
In the woodland's embrace, all worries take flight,
As the mirage of stars binds the heart to the night.

When dawn's gentle touch kisses shadows away,
The secrets of starlight begin to decay.
Yet every bright twinkle in the sky's playful sway,
Leaves echoes of magic that forever will stay.

Chasing Dreams under the Lanterned Boughs

Beneath the old boughs where the lanterns glow,
Dreams flutter gently, like leaves in the flow.
Children of twilight, with wonder ablaze,
Weaving their stories in mystical ways.

With laughter like bells, they dance through the night,
Chasing reflections of lanterns so bright.
Each step is a promise, each twirl a surprise,
As dreams take their flight in the moonlit skies.

Those lanterned branches, a gateway of hope,
Guiding young hearts as they learn how to cope.
In every warm flicker, a wish finds its voice,
And magic awakens, inviting the choice.

The night air is filled with the songs of delight,
As shadows and whispers merge into the light.
Adventure unspools from the depths of the glen,
As dreams come alive, again and again.

So gather your courage, let your spirit soar,
Under the boughs where the lanterns implore.
For in this enchanted embrace of the night,
Chasing your dreams is to truly take flight.

Glimmering Tales from the Faerie Glen

In the heart of the forest, where wonders entwine,
Glimmering tales greet those willing to pine.
Faeries whisper softly from dusk until dawn,
As the veil between worlds begins to withdraw.

With sparkles of laughter, they paint the cold air,
Telling of journeys, of love, and of care.
Each tale a treasure, wrapped in twilight's embrace,
In the Faerie Glen, where dreams find their place.

Glistening dew sits on petals anew,
While shadows of night dance in shades of deep blue.
Stories of yore, from the depths of the glen,
Awaken the echoes of magic again.

From whispers of starlight to songs of the brook,
Each moment captured, a charming little nook.
The faeries preside over realms rich and bright,
Embroidering dreams in the fabric of night.

So wander the paths where enchantments still dwell,
And listen for tales that the faeries will tell.
For in their soft murmurs, you'll find your own way,
In the glimmering world of the faerie's ballet.

Enchanted Echoes of Dappled Sunlight

In forest deep where secrets lie,
The sunlight dances, whispers shy.
Among the leaves a soft light weaves,
A tapestry of magic, it leaves.

Each shadow plays a fleeting game,
As blossoms sigh, calling your name.
With every breeze, the echoes sing,
An ancient charm on unseen wing.

Through winding paths where fairies tread,
The golden rays paint dreams unsaid.
In twilight's glow, the world awakes,
And time stands still, as magic makes.

Where sunlight dapples on the ground,
The laughter of the trees is found.
Each rustling leaf a gentle song,
An echo where our hearts belong.

So linger here, let moments blend,
In this enchanted world, my friend.
For in the glade where time does pause,
We find the magic without cause.

Radiant Whispers of the Faerie Court

Beneath the boughs of elder trees,
The faerie court hums with the breeze.
Whispers sweet like silver threads,
Weave tales of wonders long since spread.

With gossamer wings, the faeries glide,
In moonlit realms, where dreams abide.
Their laughter rings like chimes in air,
A melody found beyond despair.

Around the stones, in circle fair,
They gather close, in twilight's care.
With flickering lights, they dance aglow,
In radiant hues that softly flow.

When starlight drapes the night in gold,
Ancient stories again unfold.
With each soft murmur of the night,
The faerie court ignites delight.

So listen close, oh wandering heart,
For in their whispers, dreams impart.
A world of magic, a secret door,
Where faerie tales forever soar.

Soft Sparklines on Frosted Leaves

As morning breaks, the frost does gleam,
On leaves adorned with nature's dream.
Each sparkle bright, a work of art,
Inviting warmth to every heart.

In quiet woods, where shadows play,
The golden sun chases night away.
The frost retreats with tender grace,
Unveiling nature's secret place.

A silver touch on emerald green,
A fleeting kiss, a glimmering sheen.
In every drop, a story stirs,
Melodies sung by tiny blurs.

The whispers weave through frosty air,
A symphony beyond compare.
With every breath, a tender sigh,
As soft as dreams that pass us by.

So wander here, where magic thrives,
In diadems of nature's lives.
For in this realm, the heart will find,
A glint of joy, forever kind.

The Flickering Heart of the Elven Grove

In the elven grove, where shadows dance,
The flickering lights take their chance.
Each heartbeat pulses, vibrant and rare,
In whispers of magic that fill the air.

With every step, the spirits glow,
Guiding you softly where rivers flow.
Branches twine in a lover's embrace,
A sanctuary of time and space.

When twilight falls, the stars ignite,
Bathing the grove in ethereal light.
The flickering heart beats like a drum,
Inviting all to come, to come.

In this realm, where hope ignites,
And wonders flourish under the nights,
The elven songs drift on the breeze,
A melody whispered through trembling leaves.

So seek this place where magic thrives,
In the flickering heart, our spirit dives.
For here lies joy, in shadows cast,
A timeless realm, where dreams hold fast.

Dances of Crystalline Gossamer

In the forest where shadows play,
Gossamer threads twinkle and sway.
Fairy whispers float on the breeze,
As moonbeams twirl through ancient trees.

They dance on petals, soft and bright,
Beneath the cloak of gentle night.
With every flutter, dreams take flight,
Embracing magic wrapped in light.

A symphony of silken threads,
Where every heartbeat gently spreads.
In twilight's embrace, joy unfolds,
As stories of wonder softly told.

With laughter ringing through the air,
The world feels fresh, a banquet rare.
For every twinkle, a wish takes form,
In this realm where dreams are born.

So follow the glimmer, step by step,
Into the woods where secrets kept.
And let the dances of night inspire,
Your heart to soar, your spirit higher.

Echoes of Laughter in Sprites' Hollow

In a glade where the wildflowers bloom,
Sprites gather round, dispelling gloom.
Their laughter rings through branches high,
A melody beneath the sky.

With cheeks aglow, they spin and twirl,
Their joy is pure, their hearts unfurl.
Each echo holds a tale of old,
Of friendships penned in threads of gold.

Beneath the gaze of the watching stars,
They dance unchained, forgetting scars.
With every giggle, the night takes flight,
As shadows blend in warmed moonlight.

In Sprites' Hollow, time stands still,
A moment caught, a fleeting thrill.
For laughter is a magic rare,
That whispers softly on the air.

So venture forth, let hearts be light,
Join the revelry through the night.
And may the echoes, sweet and clear,
Guide you to joy, forever near.

Glistening Secrets Beneath the Moonlit Boughs

Underneath the boughs aglow,
Secrets whisper, soft and low.
The moon drapes silver on the ground,
While hidden treasures here abound.

In the still of night, shadows glide,
Ancient mysteries do not hide.
With gentle care, they beckon near,
To show the wonders we hold dear.

Crickets sing a soothing tune,
As stars keep watch, a bright commune.
The forest breathes, alive with grace,
Inviting all to take their place.

Each rustle speaks of tales untold,
Of dreams we chase and hearts that bold.
Beneath the boughs where magic weaves,
Glistening secrets dance like leaves.

Embrace the night, let spirits roam,
Within the woods, we find our home.
So gather close, take a deep sigh,
For in the darkness, dreams still fly.

Celestial Tapestry of Woodland Whimsy

In the heart of the whimsical wood,
Where creatures gather, misunderstood.
A tapestry of stars unfolds,
With stories spun in hues of gold.

Twilight whispers to the trees,
As breezes dance with playful ease.
Through shadows deep, adventures call,
In this enchanted, leafy hall.

The owls converse with words of lore,
While starlit paths do dream explore.
With every step, a new delight,
Unveils enchantment, warm and bright.

In woodland nooks where fairies dwell,
Each secret holds a magic spell.
And as the night wraps earth in rhyme,
The stories weave through space and time.

So lose yourself in nature's scheme,
Let whimsy guide you to your dream.
For in this realm where wonders play,
A celestial tapestry leads the way.

Hues of Magic in the Dew-Drop Dawn

Awake, the world in shimmering light,
Dewdrops sparkle like stars in flight.
Whispers of colors in gentle bloom,
Painting the edges of the softening gloom.

A breeze carries tales from the trees,
Dancing with petals, floating with ease.
Crimson and gold in a harmonious blend,
Each hue a promise that Nature will send.

A soft tingle creeps through the air,
Threads of enchantment, woven with care.
Every shadow and glint, a musical note,
Chiming together, a magical quote.

With each second, the magic unfurls,
Twisting in ribbons, like delicate swirls.
The dawn breaks gently, a tender embrace,
In the heart of the woods, a serene, sacred space.

Beneath the surface, the secrets reside,
Where magic and wonder are woven inside.
As the world awakens, breathe it all in,
The beauty of dawn, where life can begin.

Beneath the Canopy of Whispers

In the forest where secrets reside,
Ancient trees in their wisdom confide.
Branches entwined, like fingers they weave,
Stories of magic, for those who believe.

Moss carpets the ground, soft as a sigh,
Where shadows play under the vast sky.
The breeze carries murmurs from leaf to leaf,
Enticing the dreamers to spin their own belief.

Silvery beams dance on emerald glades,
Where echoes of laughter in stillness never fade.
A tapestry woven of gossamer dreams,
Drifting like whispers on silvery streams.

The magic is subtle, a flicker, a glow,
In the heart of the woods where wildflowers grow.
Each petal, a message, each fragrance, a song,
Inviting all wanderers to linger, belong.

As twilight descends, let silence be known,
For under this canopy, no one is alone.
Where hearts softly whisper and secrets unite,
Beneath the great trees, the world feels just right.

Glowing Essence of the Elders' Dance

In the twilight's embrace, where shadows align,
The elders gather, their movements divine.
Draped in the glow of the moon's silver crest,
They dance through the night, with magic expressed.

With each twirl and swirl, the air comes alive,
Spilling like nectar, sweet dreams they contrive.
Old tales take flight in a flickering blaze,
Illuminating paths through the mystic haze.

Nature holds secrets, in rhythm, they sway,
Guided by stars in the velvet array.
A circle of wisdom, of age and of grace,
Echoing laughter, time cannot erase.

The whispers of ages entwine with the night,
Breaths of the ancients, their spirits in flight.
Each flicker of fire, a heartbeat of lore,
Bringing forth magic that opens the door.

With the dawn, their dance fades into the mist,
Yet the essence remains, on the air it is kissed.
Holding the stories the forest embraced,
In the heart of the earth, their dance is interlaced.

Twilight Revelations in the Sylvan Realm

Beneath the horizon, where twilight unfolds,
The world bathes in colors, a tapestry bold.
Shadows stretch long as the stars start to peek,
Whispers of magic in silence they speak.

Night drapes her cloak, rich as the dream,
Softly the nightingale starts to redeem.
Notes flutter gently through the hushed trees,
Carving the silence with harmonious ease.

In the sylvan realm where the fae sometimes tread,
Every heartbeat a story, with each breath we're fed.
Glowing stones whisper the secrets of old,
Luminous echoes of adventures untold.

As owls take flight, with wisdom they soar,
The tapestry deepens with each breath, we explore.
Veiled in the twilight, magic sparkles anew,
Uncovering wonders in every soft hue.

And as the night deepens, let us take flight,
Through the enchanted woods, under stars shining bright.
In this realm of enchantment, forever we sway,
Where twilight reveals what daylight can't say.

Celestial Illuminations Among the Thickets

In the heart of the wood where the shadows play,
Celestial lights dance at the close of day.
Stars whisper secrets on a silver thread,
While moonbeams wrap softly, like dreams in bed.

Through the tangled thickets, soft glimmers call,
An enchantment ignites, weaving magic for all.
The night air is thick with the scent of pine,
As shadows grow long, and the owlets dine.

Every glimpse of the sky brings a shimmering sigh,
Auroras of wonder loop low and high.
The magic of twilight, so bold, so bright,
In a world hushed to listen, embracing the night.

Beneath ancient boughs where the shadows entwine,
Glorious light weaves a tale, so divine.
Each flicker a promise of stories unknown,
In the thickets of wonder, enchantments have grown.

So linger awhile in this luminous glade,
Where the stars lend their glow, and enchantments
cascade.
In celestial illuminations, our spirits take flight,
In the thickets of magic, we'll dance with the night.

Whimsy and Wonder Beneath Leafy Canopies

Beneath leafy canopies, laughter will spring,
Where whimsy and wonder take flight on a wing.
The sunbeams tangle in emerald crowns,
As secrets abound in the soft, verdant towns.

With whispers of breezes that tease at the air,
Nature inspires with wonders laid bare.
Glimmers of sunlight through branches invite,
To join in the dance of the day and the night.

Little critters weave stories of old,
In harmony stitched with threads of pure gold.
They frolic and play in the dappled glow,
Where joy becomes magic, and love starts to grow.

Curiosity blooms where imagination thrives,
As every heart stirs and every soul dives.
With each rustle and giggle, the world comes alive,
Beneath leafy canopies, our spirits will thrive.

So come to this haven where dreams find their way,
Where whimsy and wonder dance night into day.
Underneath those green arches, let adventure be free,
In a land of enchantment, just you and me.

Swaying Shadows in the Weaver's Glen

In the Weaver's Glen where shadows sway,
The tapestry whispers secrets of day.
Each thread of darkness, a story in bloom,
A dance of the twilight, a beckoning hush.

Among the tall trees, a gentle grace flows,
Swaying shadows blend in a rhythm that grows.
The heart of the forest pulses with light,
As dreams weave together, dissolving the night.

With each soft breathing of the twilight so fair,
Mysteries linger, weaving magic in air.
The moon's silver gaze glistens on dew,
Painting the glen in a soft, dreamy hue.

A symphony murmurs through thistles and ferns,
Nature's sweet secrets and soft lessons learned.
The shadows embrace, in their gentle repose,
In the Weaver's Glen, where the wild magic grows.

So linger in twilight, let your spirit take flight,
Among swaying shadows, in the stillness of night.
In the heart of the woodland, where dreams intertwine,
The Weaver's Glen beckons, a treasure divine.

A Symphony of Light Among Petal-Makers

In the garden's embrace where the petal-makers play,
A symphony of light fills the brightening day.
Each blossom a note in the music of spring,
Total harmony dances on glimmering wing.

As colors blend neatly like painters at work,
The petals swirl softly, a sweet, airy Merk.
Beneath canopies woven from flowers and leaves,
The symphony hums, as the heart gently weaves.

Sunbeams cascade, like a shower of gold,
Illuminating dreams that the garden has told.
In each fragrant whisper, in laughter, in cheer,
The symphony welcomes each soul to draw near.

The world melts away in this whimsical place,
As nature unfolds in her wondrous embrace.
Every petal a verse, every fragrance a song,
In the heart of the garden where we all belong.

So pause for a moment, let music take hold,
In the light of the petals, let stories unfold.
For a symphony plays in this magical land,
Among petal-makers, where dreams go hand in hand.

Whispers of Dappled Light

In the forest where soft shadows play,
Dappled light dances through leaves of green.
Whispers of magic in the air sway,
Nature's wonders, a serene scene.

Glimmers of hope through the branches peek,
Each ray a promise, a tale untold.
Hearts find solace, in the silence they seek,
In this tranquil realm, where joy unfolds.

Breeze carries laughter, the song of a stream,
Gentle and soothing, a melodic thread.
In petals and colors, the world finds its dream,
Where thoughts drift like clouds overhead.

Moss carpets pathways, soft underfoot,
Every step taken, a journey anew.
Within this haven, where heartbeats reshoot,
A world alive with every hue.

Embrace the stillness, breathe deep and find,
The whispers of light in the woven vines.
For in each soft shimmer, the spirits unwind,
Creating a tapestry, where magic shines.

Enchantment's Glistening Veil

Under the moon, a shimmering sight,
Veils of enchantment drape the night sky.
Stars twinkle softly, bathing in light,
Awakening dreams that learn to fly.

Crickets serenade in melodic flow,
While fireflies flicker like jewels in flight.
The world holds secrets only they know,
In this tapestry spun from the night.

Whispers of wishes ride on the breeze,
Every heartbeat a magic invoked.
As time gently pauses, hearts find their ease,
In the stories by starlight, unspoke.

Among the shadows where mysteries hide,
Lurks a charm woven deep in the dark.
Through every dark corner, wonders abide,
In dreams that ignite with a passionate spark.

So linger a little, let worries take flight,
Dance with the shadows, let laughter prevail.
For once in a while, enchantment feels right,
Under the glow of enchantment's veil.

Secrets Beneath the Starlit Canopy

Beneath the stars, where silence unfolds,
Canopies whisper of secrets untold.
Each glimmering light, a story it holds,
In the heart of the night, mysteries bold.

Branches arch low, like a guardian's embrace,
Shadows weave patterns, a delicate lace.
Footsteps are soft, as we quicken our pace,
Hoping to glimpse a forgotten face.

Crickets are crooning a timeless refrain,
While the night sky dons its velvety hue.
In the stillness, a familiar pain,
Of moments now lost, yet somehow renewed.

A flicker of stardust leads us to roam,
Exploring the realms that our hearts call home.
In the magic of night, we're never alone,
For spirits of dreams through the shadows comb.

So sit for a moment, allow the night's grace,
Trust in the magic that gathers around.
For beneath the starlit canopy's face,
A world of enchantment in silence is found.

Velvet Shadows in Emerald Glades

In emerald glades where the soft shadows lie,
Velvet whispers call from the thickets nearby.
Mysteries murmur, as the wildflowers sigh,
And time dances gently, like clouds drifting by.

Sunbeams break softly on dew-kissed ferns,
Each glowing moment, a treasure to keep.
Within this embrace, every heart learns,
To dream in the stillness, where spirits leap.

Rabbits dart lightly through thickets and briars,
While butterflies twirl in a delicate dance.
Nature's own canvas ignites our desires,
Encouraging wanderers, daring a chance.

Glistening raindrops adorn every leaf,
Reflecting magic, a world made anew.
In laughter and light, we find our belief,
In the velvet shadows with a sparkling view.

So venture forth gently, let your heart guide,
Through emerald glades, by the river so deep.
In these velvet shadows, let dreams coincide,
For the world holds its wonders for all who seek.

Wandering in the Glow of the Woodlands

In shadows deep, where secrets hide,
The flicker of dreams, a gentle guide.
Soft whispers weave through ancient trees,
A melody carried by the evening breeze.

With every step on the mossy floor,
A world awakens, forevermore.
Eyes aglow with the softest light,
The woodland beckons, a sweet delight.

Beneath the boughs, time drifts away,
In hidden glades, where shadows play.
The heart finds peace, the soul takes flight,
In tranquil realms, embraced by night.

The moonlight dances on shimmering streams,
As nature breathes in whispered dreams.
Each path unfolds a new surprise,
In the glow of the woodlands, magic lies.

So wander forth, with heart so free,
In the woodland's embrace, just you and me.
For in these woods where wonders grow,
We find ourselves in the gentle glow.

Light's Journey through the Iriswood

Through Iriswood, where colors blend,
Light wanders softly, a radiant friend.
It brushes petals with golden hue,
As secrets shimmer in morning dew.

Each beam a flicker, each shadow a sigh,
It weaves through branches, where dreams lie.
A symphony plays in the quiet morn,
As nature awakens, reborn and adorned.

In dappled glades, where spirits rise,
Sunlight dances, painting the skies.
It twirls through laughter and soft, sweet sighs,
While whispers of magic fill our eyes.

The heart of the wood sings in hues so bright,
While light's journey paints the day with delight.
With every petal, and every leaf,
Hope blossoms forth, beyond belief.

So wander through this enchanted place,
Where light and life share a warm embrace.
In the Iriswood, let your dreams take flight,
For magic is woven in the tapestry of light.

The Dance of the Wishing Willows

Beneath the boughs, where shadows play,
The wishing willows whisper and sway.
With tender grace, they reach for the sky,
In moonlit patterns, dreams drift by.

Soft rustles blend with the river's flow,
As wishes linger, the heartbeats slow.
Each tear of joy, a seed they cast,
Nurtured by whispers of futures vast.

Dancing gently, they hold our hopes,
Within their arms, the spirit copes.
For every wish thrown beneath their leaves,
A promise grows, as the heart believes.

The night is alive with the songs unsung,
As willows sway, forever young.
In this sacred grove, where dreams find ground,
The echoes of wishes are beautifully bound.

So close your eyes, let your spirit soar,
Beneath the willows, you'll find much more.
In their graceful dance, find solace and peace,
As the wishes of ages bring sweet release.

Flickering Fireflies Beneath Whispering Leaves

In the twilight haze, as stars ignite,
Fireflies flicker, bringing joy and light.
Beneath the canopy, where shadows weave,
A dance begins, by evening's leave.

Tiny lanterns in the cool night air,
With whispers soft, they weave a prayer.
Each spark a message, a heart's delight,
Illuminating dreams, banishing fright.

The leaves rustle gently, a soothing song,
As fireflies gather, where they belong.
In this enchanted cradle of night,
Every glow whispers of love's pure light.

Small wonders flit through the midnight gloom,
As nature unveils her secret bloom.
In the chorus of crickets, they play their part,
Flickering fireflies, lighting the heart.

So pause for a moment, and breathe it in,
The magic that dances, the laughter within.
For beneath whispering leaves, in shadows deep,
The flickering fireflies guard dreams we keep.

www.ingramcontent.com/pod-product-compliance
Ingram Content Group UK Ltd.
Pitfield, Milton Keynes, MK11 3LW, UK
UKHW021329280125
4330UKWH00005B/454